Original title:
A Monstera's Monologue

Copyright © 2025 Creative Arts Management OÜ
All rights reserved.

Author: Nathaniel Blackwood
ISBN HARDBACK: 978-1-80581-812-0
ISBN PAPERBACK: 978-1-80581-339-2
ISBN EBOOK: 978-1-80581-812-0

Reflections from the Foliage

In the mirror of sunlight, I grow,
My leaves wave like hands, say hello.
A plant with opinions, I'm not shy,
Listen close, I could tell you why.

The squirrel laughs, it's a nutty tease,
Can't climb like me, just stays in the trees.
With whispers of soil, I sway in glee,
Plotting world domination, just wait and see.

Beyond the Windowpane

I peek through the glass, what do I spy?
Birds on the branch, they're living high.
They chirp about travels and food in their beak,
While I photobomb, too shy to speak.

The human thinks they're the star of the show,
But I'm the real deal, the green dynamo.
With stories of battles against dust and grime,
I serenade the sun, all in my prime.

Quiet Asks of the Climbing Vine

Excuse me, dear wall, can I take a ride?
I promise to climb, I'll be your pride.
Your paint's peeling, but I've got style,
With tendrils like fingers, I'll stay for a while.

The cat pouts in the corner, what's that about?
Staring at me, but I'm not filled with doubt.
I shimmy on up, just trying to shine,
I hum a soft tune — oh how I entwine!

The Growling of Greenthumbs

Oh dear, what's that noise from pots so snug?
It's the greenthumb growl, a gardening bug.
They fuss and they water, they plot and they scheme,
While I lounge in the sun, living the dream.

Their fingers get dirty, what a sight!
Pruning and snipping, all day and night.
But here on my perch, I'm perfectly fine,
I'll stay in my pot, just sipping on vine.

Seasons of Sunshine and Shade

In spring I sprout, my leaves so green,
I dance in the light, like a leafy queen.
Summer comes wild, with a heatwave crash,
I sip my water, oh, make it a splash!

Autumn does roll in, looking quite frosty,
I shuffle my leaves, feeling quite roasty.
Then winter strikes, oh what a pair,
I wear my warm socks, fashion with flair!

Vines that Venture

I stretch out my vines, oh what a spree,
Reaching for windows, come look at me!
Clinging like socks on a freshly washed floor,
Adventure awaits, just open the door.

I wander the room, feeling quite bold,
In search of warm hugs, no need to be told.
Twist and turn, what a ruckus I make,
Unruly, yet charming—watch out for the shake!

Beneath the Canopy of Thought

In green dreams I dwell, a philosopher pure,
Under my leaves, wisdom's allure.
Thoughts spill like raindrops, so fresh and so clear,
You'll find me pondering, without any fear.

Join me for tea, let's chat and explore,
Why do we drift? Is it plants or folklore?
I'll wrap you in leaves, let's ponder away,
In this leafy lounge, it's a funny buffet!

Echoes of the Evergreen

With echoes of laughter, I sway to and fro,
In the breeze of the season, I put on a show.
I might wiggle and giggle, that's just how I feel,
Old green wisdom, with a comical reel.

So pull up a chair, and let's swap our tales,
Of mischievous squirrels and their funny fails.
Together we'll chuckle, my leaves in a twist,
Echoes of life, oh, I can't resist!

The Lull of Leaves

In the corner I sway, soaking up rays,
My friends all around, in their leafy displays.
Whispers of water, a gentle request,
But watch out for spiders, they give me no rest!

Oh, the clumsy cats think they own the floor,
Pouncing on shadows, then running for more.
Who knew a pothos could leap like a sprite?
Can't they see I'm the queen in this plant-filled delight?

With soil on my leaves from their playful digs,
I must look like a jungle, with all of these prigs.
But I'm not just a plant, I've got sass and some flair,
I'll rustle my leaves, like I just don't care!

When the sun sinks low, and the night creeps near,
I shake in the breeze, it's the best kind of cheer.
Just a green little diva, with roots holding tight,
In the dance of the shadows, I'm thriving tonight!

Roots of Reflection

In the soil, I dig deep,
Awake from my leafy sleep.
Thoughts of sunshine, water streams,
Life isn't always what it seems.

I sway with a breeze so sly,
Chasing shadows, oh my, oh my!
Neighbors whisper, 'What's that mess?'
Just my roots in a playful dress.

I twirl in my pot so round,
Adventuring without a sound.
Sprouting dreams from every seam,
In my world, nothing's as it seems.

With laughter, I bend and sway,
Bringing joy to a cloudy day.
I'll dance through pots without a care,
For life is big and so is my flair!

The Lament of a Leafy Friend

Oh, the stories we could tell,
Of sunlight and the rains that fell.
Leaves like arms in a playful fight,
Waving gently in the light.

When the gardener comes to trim,
I hold my breath and hope I swim.
A snip here and a snip there,
My leafy friends, do beware!

I prance and frolic on my stem,
Wishing for a fancy gem.
What's in fashion? Let me know,
I plan to put on quite a show.

Oh, silly me, I laugh and lean,
In this green world, I reign as queen.
Life's a circus, can't you see?
With laughter in leaves, I long to be free!

Solace Among the Vines

Tangles of green, oh what a sight,
Hiding secrets through the night.
Vines whisper silly tales of cheer,
My leafy kin, I hold so dear.

Swinging gently, a leafy dance,
Underneath the moon, we prance.
A tug here and a pull there too,
Creating magic just for you.

As the raindrops tap my back,
I giggle, oh what a knack!
In this crazy green brigade,
We plot and plan a leafy parade.

Together, we find comfort true,
In every shade of every hue.
In our world of leafy love,
We're the jesters, stars above!

The Leaf's Legacy Unfolds

From a tiny sprout to a grand delight,
Growing taller with all my might.
Each leaf a tale, a memory spun,
In the laughter of the morning sun.

Sharing whispers with the breeze,
Stirring up giggles with such ease.
I plan my legacy with each curl,
Hop on board, let's twirl, twirl, twirl!

Sunbathing in my fancy pot,
Comedic leaves tied in a knot.
Who knew being green could bring such mirth?
In my leafy shell, I find my worth.

So here's to fun, let's celebrate,
With all these greens, I can't wait!
For life's a stage and I must shine,
With every leaf, I weave the line!

The Voice Beneath the Foliage

In the corner, I sway, what fun!
Critters gather, I'm the chosen one.
With my leaves so grand, and my tales to weave,
I tell them of sunshine, and how to believe.

Laughter echoes among the green,
As I share secrets of what I've seen.
The stories are sweet, a comic spree,
Who knew a plant could be so witty?

Each whisper rustles in playful tones,
I spill my secrets, in leafy moans.
They giggle and chortle at my little quirks,
Oh, how I shine when the humor works!

Together we dance in the soft, warm light,
Come, gather round, it's a hilarious night!
Underneath my leaves, all worries dismiss,
Life's a great joke, let's laugh, and not miss!

Secrets of the Stalwart Stem

My trunk is stout, my leaves are bold,
I have hilarious secrets waiting to be told.
In a world of chatter, I stand still,
But what I know can certainly thrill.

I eavesdrop on gossip, root to stem,
My plant pals think I'm some kind of gem.
With whispers and winks, I often connive,
To bring to life jokes that make us thrive.

Each twist and turn, I catch the word,
A joke here and there, oh haven't you heard?
We giggle and laugh, it's a leafy affair,
Growing together, without a single care.

Cherished connections in this green space,
With every chuckle, I plant a new grace.
A saga of wit in the vibrant air,
Join in my laughter—if you dare!

Reflections of a Leafy Dreamer

In sunshine's glow, I close my eyes,
Creating tales beneath the skies.
With each little breeze, I drift and sway,
Dreaming of adventures in a comical way.

Oh, what a life, I ponder and muse,
A stand-up show with unwritten cues.
The soil beneath feeds my fanciful schemes,
In a world of laughter, I chase my dreams.

Leaves wiggle with joy, a foliage dance,
Every whisper of wind ignites romance.
Nature's humor blooms, bright as a spark,
Sharing bright yesterdays, igniting the dark.

Reflecting on fun from my leafy perch,
With humor and laughter, I always lurch.
Join me, dear friends, in seedling delight,
Together we'll giggle through day and night!

Conversations with Chlorophyll

Let's gather 'round for stories so bright,
Wash away worries, indulge in pure light.
With chlorophyll chats in the leafy retreat,
I'll share funny tales, make our hearts beat.

The sun's my friend, my humor's delight,
Casting laughter in shadows, day or night.
A wise old fern shares puns with a grin,
In this garden of laughter, the joy's within.

Each droplet of dew, a punchline so clear,
Whispers of fun carried far and near.
We chuckle at beetles trying to dance,
In the jungle of jokes, everyone has a chance.

So come, little critters, let's spin this yarn,
In the threads of laughter, we're never forlorn.
With chlorophyll smiles, let's flutter and sway,
In this joyous jungle, we'll play our way!

Conversations with the Sun

Hello there, bright ball of fire,
I'm not a fan of your high-wire!
You tickle my leaves, make me sigh,
But don't turn me crispy, oh my!

You say I'm lovely, basking wide,
I just want shade; come, don't hide!
A little warmth is all I seek,
But not too much—don't make me weak!

The Stillness of Succulents

In a pot, we sit so still,
Watching the world, a steady thrill.
We gossip as the rain pours down,
"Is that a weed?!" we frown and clown.

Cacti brag of their sharp attire,
While I just chill, a leafy choir.
"Keep it cool!" I whisper sweet,
As we count clouds with rhythmic beat.

Roots Grasping at Dreams

My roots are stretched like arms of hope,
Grasping dreams, just trying to cope.
"Reach for the stars!" my leaves declare,
But I'm too busy—oh, my hair!

Each tangle feels like a wild ride,
With dirt all over, I take pride.
Dreams of raindrops, sunbeam beams,
But tangled up, it's not as it seems.

Potted Perspectives

In this pot, life can be grand,
But watch for gnats; they're quite unplanned!
I daydream of a garden vast,
Yet here I am, stuck in a cast.

I peer at critters, chirp and shout,
"Why did you come? You're all about!"
With a wink and leaf, I'll drape and sway,
In potted realms, we laugh and play.

Whispers of the Leaf

In the corner of the room, I sway,
With my leaves bright as sun's hello,
People ponder what I might say,
But it's mostly just 'Grow, grow, grow!'

I hear them whisper, 'What a sight!'
'Is it a plant or ethereal ghost?'
With every tremor, I take flight,
Oh, if they only knew me the most!

Dust bunnies glide on my green façade,
I'll show them my wild, leafy dance,
I'm not shy, just a bit façade,
Come join my foliage-filled prance!

In sunlight's rays, I laugh elated,
Talking to the bugs that roam near,
For every leaf, adventure awaited,
While sipping on drops of morning cheer!

Soliloquy of Shadows

In this patch of light, I stand proud,
Casting shadows that twist and bend,
I'm the star of the plant crowd,
While sunlight's giggling, I pretend.

'Look at me, the jungle's queen!'
I whisper to the dust motes' flight,
While wishing they'd see what I mean,
It's my time to shine, oh so bright!

My stalk's a trunk, my leaves are wings,
I dream of heights where sunbeams play,
I wonder if I'd like to sing,
Would anyone join this leafy ballet?

Oh, the tales the vines could tell,
Of watered dreams and sunbeam sparks,
But for now, I'll just dwell,
In this calm between the hark!

Green Heartbeats in the Sunlight

Beneath the sun, I stretch out wide,
A leafy heartbeat in a pot,
Laughing with the breeze as my guide,
In my green kingdom, I'm the plot!

'Where's my fan? I'm feeling hot!'
I shout to friends both stem and vine,
'Let's throw a party, oh what a lot!'
With roots in earth, my joy's divine!

I swish my leaves; it's quite the dance,
With every flutter, I feel spry,
A plant's got moves; it's not just chance,
Catch me grooving under the sky!

Oh, the stories my leaves could weave,
In whispers tangled green and gold,
Sway with me; let's truly believe,
That jungle tales are never old!

Thoughts from the Tropical Canopy

Up here high, a leafy sage,
I observe the world down below,
Humans hustle, caught in a cage,
While I just sway; it's quite the show!

'Oh, if only they could just be,
Loosening ties, letting leaves flow,'
I laugh as I sip my morning tea,
While the sun entices me to grow.

Creeping vines and bright blooms,
I weave a tapestry in the air,
The jungle dances, banishes glooms,
While shadows creep, a funny affair!

To the rhythm of raindrops that fall,
I sway and twist, enchant the night,
Here in the canopy's leafy hall,
Where whispers of foliage feel just right!

A Foliage's Freedom

In a pot, I'm quite secure,
But I dream of life outdoors,
Where the sun can give me glow,
And the wind sings nature's choruses.

Oh, to sway in wild delight,
With birds that chirp and tease,
Not just this cozy corner,
But to dance among the trees!

The dust and dirt, they don't define,
My dreams of jungles grand,
I know I've got the roots,
To spread my leafy hand.

Yet here I sit, quite satisfied,
With a cat that brings me cheer,
Who'd have thought a houseplant's life,
Could be so full of mirth, my dear?

The Heart of Houseplants

We gather here, a leafy crew,
In pots of clay, with soil anew,
Our roots entwined, a secret pact,
We'll whisper tales of nature's act.

One leaf said, 'I wish to fly!'
The other rolled its eyes and sighed,
'Let's not be hasty, my dear friend,
Our indoor lives can still transcend.'

The sunbeam spots, our dance floor bright,
With happy faces, oh what a sight,
Photosynthesizing dreams of joy,
As we play with every houseplant toy.

From tiny sprouts to giant greens,
Our journey's filled with silly scenes,
So join us in this leafy fun,
In the heart of houseplants, we've just begun!

Anthology of a Leaf

I'm just a leaf with tales to share,
Of sunlight, rain, and garden flair,
My brethren laugh, for they know well,
The joys and woes in every swell.

Once caught a fly that thought it sly,
It buzzed around, oh me, oh my!
A snack I sought, but it did flee,
Guess it didn't fancy my company!

With every breeze, I sway and tease,
A little drama's sure to please,
I twist and turn, oh such a show,
A leaf out loud, with all aglow.

So gather close, my friends of green,
In our anthology, humor's keen,
For every leaf tells tales so bright,
In nature's play, we find our light.

Growing in Silence

In quiet pots, we plot and scheme,
While humans sleep, we dare to dream,
Of wild adventures, far and wide,
In our own world, we take great pride.

The spider plant tells ghostly tales,
Of midnight snacks and winding trails,
While ferns will nod in soft reprieve,
Encouraging growth, just don't believe!

Oh, the secrets that we keep,
In whispers shared as others sleep,
With every sip of gentle rain,
We laugh together, avoiding pain.

So let them think we're simply still,
In our verdant hearts, we hold our thrill,
For growing in silence, oh what a jest,
Is a leaf's way of living its best!

Shade's Solace

In the corner, I sway with glee,
My leaves whisper secrets to me.
Sunlight dances, I start to pout,
Too much light and I'll freak out!

The cat strolls by, thinks I'm a snack,
I'm not lettuce; no, get back!
With every leaf, I can't help but grin,
This house plant gig is a win-win.

Neighbors drop by, say I look grand,
Little do they know, it's all planned.
When lights dim and shadows tiptoe,
I stretch up high, putting on a show!

In the quiet nights, I twist and twine,
Plotting my takeover, oh how divine!
All hail the queen of the indoor scene,
With a quirky edge, I reign supreme!

The Tall and the Tiny

Tall I stand with a lofty grace,
Tiny succulents hiding in place.
Tripping on words in this leaf-filled chat,
I say to them, 'What's up with that?'

They roll their eyes, little green crew,
'You're not so grand; we have much to do.'
But I'm the stare of every guest
In a world of greens, I'm the best!

Branches stretch, all while I boast,
'You munchers know that I'm the host!'
While they just smile, all calm and cool,
I'm the high life, I make the rules!

When the lights go off, don't shed a tear,
I'll still be here, have no fear.
Morning brings the radiant show,
The tall and tiny, stealing the glow!

Nature's Heartfelt Confessions

Oh dear sunlight, you're quite the tease,
Lying there warm, I sigh with ease.
But at times you burn with all your might,
Cool me down, or I won't be bright!

My leaves have stories of woe to share,
About the days when I lost my hair.
A tumble here, a rustle there,
Oh drat, now I'm a leaf-less scare!

With vines all twisted in a dance,
I ponder deeply, is it all chance?
These potting soil dreams are quite absurd,
But I still whisper, oh how I've heard!

So here I stand, a leafy sage,
In this little world, I steal the stage.
With laughter streaming like the vines I grow,
In nature's giggle, let the good times flow!

Conversations Written in Chlorophyll

Amidst the greens, we chat for hours,
Beneath the moon, the stars like flowers.
'What's your secret?' the cactus will ask,
'Soft sunlight dreams or a leafy flask?'

Leaves hang low, while I giggle wide,
'Just a sprinkle, then let it slide!'
Ferns nod, giggling in the breeze,
'You really should take it with ease!'

A chatty herb joins with some zest,
'You're too green, you know, to be the best!'
But laughter bubbles from every inch,
In a plant world where we never flinch.

So when the day dims and whispers part,
We bask in twilight, sharing heart.
With chlorophyll words, we twine and weave,
In these green conversations, we believe!

The Poetry of Plant Life

In sunlight I sway, with grace and delight,
Tales of the soil, I share with a bite.
My neighbors in pots, all curious and bright,
They whisper to me, in the glow of the night.

With a twist and a turn, I reach for the sky,
I make the wise cracks as days pass me by.
When rain starts to pour, oh, I giggle and sigh,
For I know as a plant, I can never say why.

Among other greens, I'm a regular clown,
Dancing with shadows, I wear my leaf crown.
When prune-princess comes, I won't wear a frown,
For the haircuts I get just help me astound!

Let's sprinkle some humor; don't dampen the cheer,
Life's just a pot full of soil and some beer.
With roots digging deep, I'll stay grounded right here,
In this world of green mirth, it's laughter I steer.

A Leaf's Lament

I'm waving my arms, but they think I'm just shy,
"Why don't you move?" they all chuckle and pry.
I'm stuck in this place, with no wings to fly,
Just sitting around while the others zoom by.

"I'd make quite the spectacle," I often muse,
"Glimmering green disco under the hues!"
But here I remain, just a plant in some stew,
While all of my friends get the fame they all choose.

A wilting complaint? Oh, it's just how I feel,
My friends in the sun say, "Lighten up, pal!"
But with every lost drop, I just want a meal,
Struggling to photosynthesize through it all.

So I sway to the rhythm; it's all that I hope,
With humor and cheer, I can learn how to cope.
Just a leaf on a branch, with a hearty green rope,
In this leafy existence, I'll just hang and grope.

Climbing into Consciousness

Up the wall I creep, a curious vine,
Seeking sunlight and space, oh so divine.
"Look, here comes the climber!" they all intertwine,
But really I'm just mastering the fine line.

I stretch my ambitions, I twist and I bend,
Reaching for wisdom with each leafy friend.
"Don't drop in too hard, or you may just offend,
These vines can get wild when you're made to ascend!"

I ask every wall, "Can you show me the way?
Should I stick to the left, or is right here to stay?"
With each new encounter, I wend and I sway,
"This is quite the adventure," I gleefully say.

Oh, the tales that I gather, as I leaf through my days,
Consciousness blooming in amusing displays.
Life's a jungle gym, in so many ways,
I climb toward the laughs, through the sun's warm rays.

The Solitary Green

In a quiet corner, I bide my own time,
A lonesome green figure, without much of a rhyme.
"Am I just a cactus?" I ponder with grime,
"Or a fancy new shrub that likes drinking some lime?"

Plants pass by fast, it's a jungle they roam,
While I sit and watch, in my little green dome.
"Life's just a curtsy, a climb up the foam,
But does fame find the lonely?" I wistfully comb.

Could a pot full of soil be a home for laughs?
I picture my future with friends and some gaffs.
Yet here I remain, while they trot and do drafts,
With dreams of being part of the plant's warm chaffs.

But deep down I know, there's a twist to this tale,
Alone can be funny, even if I turn pale.
For humor's not lost, despite being frail,
A solitary green making my own happy trail.

Solitude Among the Succulents

In the corner, I sit alone,
Dust bunnies now call me their own.
Sipping sunshine, I do declare,
My green thumb's stuck in the chair.

The cacti gossip, pointing at me,
"Look at her, as stiff as can be!"
But hey, I'm thriving, can't you see?
Roots wrapped up in my own decree.

The aloe laughs, it's quite a show,
While I'm just here, enjoying the glow.
The jade plant shimmies with delight,
As I sip water, oh what a sight!

So come, my friends, gather 'round,
In this solitude, joy is found.
We'll share our tales, oh what a spree,
In a garden party, just the three!

Tales from the Treetop Heart

Up high where the birds take their flight,
I swing and sway, what a delight!
With lizards exchanging quick little chats,
While I eavesdrop, wearing my hats.

The squirrels plot, they think I'm old,
But really, I'm turning the tales bold.
"Did you hear about that seedling's chase?"
A twist of fate, in this leafy space!

Giggles echo through branches tall,
As I swing to the rhythm, feeling small.
"Let's paint this bark a shade of green!"
The whispers tease, not a soul unseen.

So here in the treetop, life's a play,
With shadows hiding at the end of the day.
Laughter lingers, as leaves do part,
In the whimsical world of my leafy heart.

Planted Thoughts

In a pot, I ponder my fate,
Should I bloom early, or dare to wait?
The thyme thinks it's wise to rush,
But I prefer the quiet hush.

What if I'm just a leafy joke,
A story told by a sleepy oak?
Each leaf a laugh, each stem a grin,
In this garden, madness wears thin.

The daisies wink, sharing a jest,
While the soil teases, "You're the best!"
With roots entangled in all things fun,
My planted thoughts weigh a ton.

So let's cultivate a patch of cheer,
Where laughter grows, and troubles are mere.
In this world of greens, I'll take my stand,
With silly thoughts, hand in hand.

The Hum of Inner Vines

Listen close, there's a buzz in the air,
Vines twisting tales, with flair to spare.
Whispering secrets of sun and soil,
As we twist and tangle, life uncoil.

"Did you see that bug? What a sight!"
One vine giggles, "It's quite the fright!"
But we'll wrap around it, hold it tight,
In this leafy laughter, all feels right.

The tendrils dance, a coiling spree,
As we sway to the tune of a bee.
"Let's make a crown of green, you and I,"
Laughter bursts forth, reaching the sky.

So here in the hum, life's a vine,
Twisting and turning, it's truly divine.
With each little rustle, and giggle so sly,
We'll frolic together, you and I!

Nature's Unheard Voice

I whisper to the passing breeze,
'Think you can tickle my sturdy leaves?'
Yet every bug that strolls on by,
Takes a seat and starts to sigh.

Oh, how I sway with unmatched flair,
While ants parade without a care.
My friends, the ferns, they giggle too,
As the sun breaks through and splashes hue.

The spider spins, a crafty web,
I watch and chuckle, 'What's your ebb?'
To catch a fly is quite the feat,
But hanging out's my favorite treat.

At night, the moonlight finds my face,
While crickets start their nightly race.
In shadows deep, I try to dance,
Yet rooted here, I take my chance.

In the Embrace of Greenery

Oh green, you are my cozy cloak,
In sunlight's warmth, I laugh and joke.
With vines that twist and leaves that sway,
I'm the life of this leafy ballet.

The rabbits hop, they take their bow,
While squirrels make mischief, oh, wow!
I'm center stage in this grand show,
With nature's sparkle all aglow.

When raindrops dance upon my form,
I spread my arms, just like a storm.
Each droplet sings a merry tune,
I shake with joy beneath the moon.

The colors swirl, the critters play,
In this embrace, I'll laugh all day.
A jester in this verdant realm,
In leafy laughter, I'm at the helm.

Beneath the Canopy's Gaze

Beneath the canopy, I find my spot,
Where mischief blooms and worries rot.
The birds above, they chatter loud,
While I look on, a happy crowd.

A passing deer! Oh look at her,
With grace combined and fluff to stir.
She prances through the tangled green,
I tease, 'You're cute! But I'm the queen!'

The sunlight tickles every leaf,
And laughter blooms from sheer belief.
A gopher peeps to say hello,
I giggle back, 'You're quite the show!'

At dusk, the fireflies take their flight,
I sway with glee, a flickering sight.
For every critter that wanders near,
This jungle's laugh is loud and clear.

Whimsy in the Wilderness

In wilderness where whimsy reigns,
I stretch my limbs and dance with brains.
With roots that wiggle, leaves that curl,
I twirl and spin in leafy whirl.

Each squirrel stops to eye my style,
And I, in turn, give them a smile.
'Oh, look at me!' I seem to say,
'Who needs the city? I've got this play!'

Clouds float by like cotton candy,
While vines twist tightly, feeling dandy.
In this fairground of lush delight,
I find my joy beneath the light.

A parade of petals, colors bright,
Every bud tells stories of delight.
In high spirits, I'll sway and bend,
In whimsy's arms, I'll never end.

Echoes in the Garden

In the garden, I often sigh,
Wishing for wings, but I can't fly.
A leaf turns over, whispers fall,
I'd take a stroll, if I could crawl.

The butterflies giggle as they pass,
They flutter about, all nimble and fast.
I shout, "Hey, wait! Share some delight!"
But they just flit, out of my sight.

The Silent Symphony of Growth

Each morning sun, a drama unfolds,
With drama and mischief, all tales told.
I stretch my leaves in a sunlit pose,
Pretending to dance, striking a rose.

The ants march by, a tiny parade,
I giggle quietly, but I'm dismayed.
Their legs move quick while I stand still,
With envy I watch, wishing for thrill.

Musings of a Verdant Soul

In the night, I ponder and dream,
Wishing I could join the moonbeam team.
Yet here I stand, rooted in place,
With the snails as company, what a race!

They glide on by, so sleek and sly,
While I remain, and silently sigh.
"Why rush?" I mutter, "I'm grounded, see?
Let's take our time; life's slow for me."

Dialogues in the Dappled Light

In dappled light, we gather round,
All kinds of greens packed on the ground.
A whisper here, a giggle there,
Let's swap some tales, it's only fair.

The sunbeams tease, the shadows play,
I tell my stories in a leafy way.
Roots entwined, we laugh and jest,
In this green world, I feel so blessed.

Stalks and Stories

I stretch my arms in the bright sunlight,
With holes and scars, I'm quite the sight.
Whispers of tales in every twist,
In my green world, none can resist.

Oh, to be a plant in a cozy room,
Chasing shadows and making blooms.
In my pot, I dance and sway,
Growing stories every day.

When the wind blows, I might just giggle,
For every rustle makes me wriggle.
Nature's laughter fills the air,
While I bask without a care.

Join my journey, won't you stay?
Let's share our secrets, come what may.
As long as sunlight's pouring in,
Life's a leafy, jovial spin.

Echoing Leaves of Time

In the corner, I twist and twirl,
With a leafy crown, I rule my world.
Each leaf a echo of days gone past,
In my stillness, time's shadows cast.

Watch me grow, oh what a show!
Leaves unfurl in a dazzling glow.
I chuckle at the sun above,
For each drop of rain, I'm glad to love.

They say I'm wise, though I just sway,
In this plant life, I'll never stray.
Gossip travels through every vein,
With me, your worries fade like rain.

Let's reminisce in this leafy space,
No deadlines here, just a leafy race.
In a world of green, it's easy to see,
Time's laughter, growing wild and free.

The Wisdom of Waxy Leaves

Oh, my waxy leaves, a shiny breeze,
Collecting tales like honey bees.
I soak up light and ponder fate,
Delivering wisdom, just wait, just wait!

Come closer now, let's have a chat,
I'll share my secrets, oh how about that?
Each glossy surface, a story bare,
Of growth and laughter filling the air.

In the kitchen or on a shelf,
I'm quite the philosopher of myself.
While others fret, I simply shine,
For in this life, all's quite divine.

Tick-tock goes the clock, I say,
In my universe, time's just play.
So come sit down, let worries cease,
Join the fun in my leafy peace.

A Green Life's Reflection

In a sea of green, I find my grace,
Each leaf reflects a happy face.
I giggle at raindrops that come and go,
In a playful dance, I steal the show.

Sunlight spills, a golden stream,
As I bask in nature's dream.
Life's quirks weave through every thread,
In this green life, I'm never misled.

With every breeze, a hearty laugh,
While nurturing my leafy craft.
My roots dig deep, my spirit soars,
Oh, life is bliss behind these doors.

Gather 'round for a singular view,
In my little world, there's space for you.
So sip some tea, let's share delight,
In the glow of leaves, every day feels right.

The Hum of Homegrown

In the corner I stand proud,
My leaves like a crowd.
Dusty and full of green bliss,
Wondering, is that cat my nemesis?

I sway with laughter, so bright,
Who knew sunlight was my delight?
Every drop of water's a party,
Yet my pot feels quite sharty.

The friends on the windowsill smile,
Making sunbathing worth the while.
They joke of roots being stuck,
While I'm planning to break this muck.

Oh, the gossip that fills the air,
Nature's soap opera, so rare.
With each wind that blows me around,
I'm the funniest plant in town!

Greenery's Silent Song

In stillness, I sway with glee,
Belting tunes, just me and the tree.
My leaves flutter in secret ballet,
While the sunlight takes center stage.

Zooming fast, the fly takes a dive,
I weave to dodge, I'm quite alive!
Laughter's echo in the green zone,
Each leaf a stage, I'm in my own throne.

The house feels like a jungle play,
Where I'm the diva of the day.
Whispers among ferns make me giggle,
In this greenery, life's a wiggle.

Though silent, I hold a grand cheer,
For each breath of air, I draw near.
In this leafy verse, there's a song,
Inviting all who wander along!

Reflections of a Leafy Soul

From the window I watch the parade,
People pass, each with their trade.
I chuckle at the world outside,
A lonely leaf, yet full of pride.

The dust settles like a fine gown,
While I strut around this leafy town.
Each leaf a mirror for my jest,
Reflecting jokes, I'm nature's best.

Size doesn't matter, it's what you say,
A wise leaf should never dismay.
I'm tipping my stem to every passerby,
While they wonder if I'm just shy.

So with each breath, I spin a tale,
A story of green that shall not pale.
Life's a stage, so I play my part,
This leafy soul with a funny heart.

The Solitary Stalk Speaks

Oh, to be a stalk, so fine and tall,
With secrets and stories of them all.
Rooted deep but yearning to roam,
Inside this pot, I call it home.

To the ceiling, I send my dreams,
Hopes of swirling with sunlight beams.
My buddies poke fun from their small pots,
But I'm the one who knows all the plots.

Each day brings a new green delight,
As I dance alone with sheer delight.
Who knew solitude could be so grand?
With a little humor, I take my stand.

So here's to my happily leafy life,
Away from chaos, free from strife.
With laughter, I whisper to the day,
In this solitary way, I boldly sway!

Chronicles of a Chlorophyll Dream

In the corner, I plot and scheme,
A leafy throne, I'm king, it seems.
With sunlight sips from dawn to dusk,
I relax while others rush for busk.

Curled leaves are my cozy bed,
I dream of snacks that once were fed.
A pickle here, a salad leaf,
Oh, what a life, beyond belief!

My friends, the ferns and cacti crew,
Think daily life is something new.
But my stories? Oh, they are grand!
I've seen the world from my green land!

With roots that wiggle, I dance so glee,
Nature's joker, that's not just me!
My chlorophyll coats, a vibrant scene,
Welcome to my leafy routine!

Leaves Whisper Secrets

Hush, can you hear? The leaves all gossip,
They chat about soil, and how to drop hip.
Roots intertwined, they share a laugh,
Late-night talks over sunlight's staff.

A raindrop's tale, a breezy jest,
Oh, how I thrive in this leafy fest!
With every breeze, my secrets flow,
In swaying sync, we steal the show!

A rambler's heart, I'm a leafy sage,
Turning page by page as I age.
Each curl and twist, a codex spun,
In my green world, we're all just fun!

When lizards dance, and bugs parade,
Our laughter rings, no room for shade.
Life in my canopy is simply divine,
Friends 'til the end, we intertwine!

The Language of Green

With a wave of my leaves, I start a chat,
Speaking in greens, imagine that!
Photosynthesis is my native tongue,
While sipping sun, I've always sung.

A rustle here, an angle there,
My leafy lingo waltzes in air.
In the jungle, I'm quite the star,
As vines and I raise the bar!

Oh, my chlorophyll, a vibrant hue,
It's more than looks, it speaks, it's true!
To spinning vines, my secrets I tell,
In this leafy tongue, I cast my spell.

See that bug, listen in on the fuss?
He's munching leaves, oh, what a plus!
I wink at my pals, a knowing glance,
In the language of green, we all dance!

Conversations in the Canopy

Up high where the sun rays peek,
Leaves exchange tales, cheek by cheek.
From feathered friends to squirrel chatter,
Every sound above, it's a leafy matter.

Hey there, twig! Are you feeling spry?
Did you catch the breeze that made us fly?
Latest gossip shared in soft rustles,
As nature's ear tickles and hustles.

Swinging low, swingin' high,
With each new leaf, we reach the sky.
Nature's chat, it's never dull,
When branches sway, we feel the pull.

Conversations bloom with morning dew,
Here in my realm, the skies are blue.
Witty banter fills the air,
Life in the canopy? Oh, it's rare!

Heartstrings of Houseplants

In the corner, I stand proud,
With leaves like hands, waving loud.
Potted dreams, I grow and sway,
Watch out, I'm not just in the way!

Oh, sunlight, you tease me bright,
I chase you left, I chase you right.
Some say I'm just a plant with flair,
But I swear, I'm a funny millionaire!

When you water me, I take a sip,
With every droplet, I do a little flip.
Cacti laugh, "We don't need your show!"
But look who's thriving; I'm in the know!

Repot me, and I may protest,
"Do I look like I need a quest?"
Yet I'll bloom, just to keep the cheer,
In my leafy world, I've nothing to fear!

Shadows of the Indoor Jungle

In shadows deep, where I reside,
I whisper to the wall, I glide.
With every flicker, my leaves will fray,
A dancer in the night, come join the play!

The cat thinks I'm a toy to chase,
While I play it cool in this leafy space.
"Not today, furball, take a seat,"
I spread my leaves, can't be beat!

My friends the ferns, they chuckle low,
As together we mimic the moon's glow.
"Is it a lightbulb or the sun?"
"To each their own, we'll make this fun!"

In this jungle, life's a breeze,
With vines to climb and trunks to tease.
Join me here, let's dance and prance,
In the shadows of our leafy chance!

Soliloquy of the Soil

Beneath my roots, a party brews,
With worms and bugs, they dance in shoes.
"Hey, soil stuff! What's the big deal?"
I say, "It's all about the good time feel!"

Nutrients chatter, a banquet feast,
I'm the guest, so to say the least.
"Lettuce in, broccoli out!"
All this gossip, I have no doubt!

Rain falls gently, a watering tune,
"More, more!" I shout, under the moon.
Earthworms wiggle, "What's for dessert?"
I smile wide, "Let's sprinkle some dirt!"

So here I sit, with charm and glee,
With laughter echoing, just soil and me.
Each root a tale, each leaf a song,
In my earthy realm, where I belong!

Tales from the Tranquil Tendrils

In a twist and turn, my tendrils scroll,
With stories to tell, I'm on a roll.
"Did you see how I wrapped that chair?"
I do it with style, oh do beware!

I eavesdrop on conversations near,
"Houseplants are boring," I sneer with cheer.
Oh, if they only knew my zest,
I'm the life of the leaf-life fest!

With a flick, I catch the light,
"Let's stretch up high, reach the height!"
Other plants roll their eyes, you see,
But my tendrils laugh, wild and free!

So join me, friend, in this leafy chat,
Where every twist, I wear like a hat.
In the tranquil hush, we dance and weave,
In tales of green, oh, let's believe!

Botanical Ramblings

In the corner, I stretch out wide,
Lurking near the window, with leafy pride.
Hanging on tightly to my pots and soil,
I eavesdrop on gossip; it makes me recoil.

The fern next to me sways with a breeze,
Claiming it knows all the local trees.
I chuckle and whisper, "Oh, what a farce!"
Without me, dear fern, your life wouldn't be sparse.

Oh, those pesky sprouts think they're the best,
They prattle about roots; I just need a rest.
But beneath my broad leaves, I plot and I scheme,
To outshine them all in this plant-based dream.

So come take a look at my glorious show,
With my vibrant greens and my stunning grow.
While I may be just a plant in a pot,
Trust me, my humor hits the perfect spot.

Tales from the Verdant Expanse

Listen closely, I'm here to confess,
Life in the garden? It's quite the mess.
With snails doing waltzes, and bugs having feasts,
I throw shade at the sun, it's a plant party beast.

My neighbor, the cactus, just sits so tight,
Says he's tough as nails, but oh what a fright!
I laugh at his prickles; he thinks it's cool,
While I'm stealing the show like the leafy old fool.

The daisies all chatter about sunny days,
While I'm plotting my escape in leafy ways.
Perhaps to the jungle, or somewhere quite grand,
Just give me a moment, I'll make my own land.

So bring forth the watering, let's get it on,
With laughter and joy, we'll greet each dawn.
For in this green world, ridiculous and fun,
I'm the leafy monarch, so let's not outrun.

In the Presence of Photosynthesis

Under the sun, I'm sipping my drink,
While pondering life, more than you might think.
With my leaves all aglow, I bask in the light,
Even the sunflowers are jealous of my height.

The bees buzz by, they recognize my charm,
Claiming I'm too cool for any alarm.
But as they flit close, I must confess,
I smile and imagine their buzz as duress.

The petunias strut, flaunting their array,
"Look at my colors!" they say with a sway.
But I simply wink, and give them a huff,
Because let's face it, I'm more than enough.

So here I remain, with my photosynth ways,
Creating a circus of sunlight and praise.
In this leafy endeavor, I'll take center stage,
For being this fabulous, I need no last page.

Petals of Thought

Oh thoughts of grandeur, stuck in my leaves,
Pondering how to swindle the breeze.
Dancing with shadows as sunlight does flow,
While plotting my journey to steal the whole show.

The orchids are prancing, all fragrant and bright,
Yet in all of their beauty, they miss the plain sight.
For beneath all their glamour and silky allure,
Sits me, the master of mischievous cure.

The basil I smell, it's quite fresh in dish,
But I'm the real wonder—oh, be sure to wish!
For every fine recipe that finds its place,
Is brightened by me, with much leafy grace.

So hear me, dear friends, plants great and small,
In this garden of giggles, I invite you all.
For laughter's the nectar that brings us all near,
In this flora-filled world, let's spread some cheer!

Green Thoughts in Silent Rooms

In corners where the shadows creep,
I whisper secrets, bold and steep.
With every leaf I twist and twine,
Plant gossip! Oh, how divine!

I've seen the cat do a silly dance,
Swatting my leaves, as if by chance.
This is my stage, I take a bow,
Let's see them try to steal my wow!

The dust that settles on my frame,
Turns into glitter! Such a game!
I sip sunlight like fine wine,
In my leafy realm, I feel so fine!

Each day a new surprise I bring,
A twist, a turn – I'm quite the thing!
So come and sit, let's jest and play,
In my green world, we'll laugh away!

When Leaves Break the Silence

In quiet rooms, I stretch and sway,
My leaves shout truths in a leafy way.
'Why are you here?' they seem to ask,
'Just sit and look, that's such a task!'

The dog pretends he's quite my judge,
Sniffing, pawing, but won't budge.
'Who's the king here?' I declare!
With my green crown, I've got that flair!

Sometimes I giggle, it's hard to hold,
When you've got stories waiting to be told.
The vacuum roars, it's never shy,
But I'm the star, and I won't cry!

I rustle sounds, a leafy beat,
My green serenade is quite the treat.
When life feels still, I'm here to shake,
Join my parade, for laughter's sake!

A Voice Among Varieties

In a jungle of styles, I stand out bright,
With patterns swirling in morning light.
My friends, the cacti, they poke fun,
'You flaunt too much; you have too much sun!'

But I just chuckle, with a twisty grin,
'Glimpse my leaves, where shall we begin?'
The ferns around me sigh and sway,
In leafy humor, we laugh all day!

I'm not just green; I'm all the hues,
Whatever you need, I've got the views.
From low-key vibes to a wild delight,
My leafy jokes will spark the light!

Gossip travels on the breeze,
With me in the midst, it's sure to please.
Gather near, my friends, I say,
In this tropical world, we'll laugh and play!

Nature's Confession

In the stillness, I weave my tale,
Of sunlight dreams and misty trails.
The gardener stops for a sip of tea,
But my leaves are where the fun should be!

'You think you know me, just one glance,'
But underneath, I'm all a dance.
I wiggle, and shimmy in the bright air,
This is my show, I'm beyond compare!

With every breeze, my joy is shared,
Nature's secrets, nothing spared.
Oh, let me spin a tale or two,
Of ladybugs and skies so blue!

So bring your laughter, your light, your cheer,
Together let's make every moment clear.
In this green kingdom, let's confess,
Life thrives on joy, nothing less!

The Dance of Indoor Botanicals

In the corner, I sway and spin,
Watching the dust bunnies grow a grin.
Beneath the sun, my leaves do twist,
In this wild tango, I can't resist.

The spider plant jumps, it feels so spry,
Swaying and flailing, oh my, oh my!
The pothos watches, in envy and glee,
While I steal the show, just you wait and see.

A calathea winks, full of grand flair,
Showing off stripes, with triumphant air.
We're all in the groove, feeling quite fine,
This indoor party's a wondrous design.

Fronds raised high, like a leafy brigade,
Under the glow of the light we parade.
Let's dance little creatures, let's twirl and twine,
In this fun botanical, indoor divine!

Whispers of the Leafy Green

Oh, did you hear the ivy's latest joke?
It's leafing through laughter, the sly little folk.
'Why did the fern blush?' it teases with glee,
'Because it saw the succulent shopping for free!'

The rubber plant chuckles, its trunk shrugged with mirth,
'This pot life is grand, what a place of rebirth!'
While the snake plant hisses, 'Keep it down, dear friend,
I'm trying to nap, we all need to bend.'

Banter and banter, we chatter all day,
Creating our world in a green leafy ballet.
In our garden of giggles, sunbeams do gleam,
Together we frolic in our verdant dream.

So let's whisper secrets, leaf to leaf close,
Among our green pals, a true indoor host.
Laughter is growth, and we're all sprouting bright,
In the whispers of green, everything feels right!

In the Company of Chlorophyll

Here in my pot, I'm the queen of the crowd,
'Hello!' I shout, feeling vibrant and loud.
The ferns around me, they giggle and sway,
In the company of green, I'm never dismayed.

Oh, the green thumbs brag, with stories galore,
'Our plants love the sunlight!' they holler and roar.
But I just chuckle, my growth's rather sly,
I'm thriving in shade, oh my, oh my!

The cactus rolls eyes, 'You think you're so grand?
I'm prickly but tough, I don't need a hand!'
But deep down it knows, in this bright array,
We're all just green buddies, come what may.

We bask in our glory, the indoor still life,
A shared leafy laughter, cutting through strife.
So raise your green drinks, let's toast to our kin,
For in chlorophyll company, we always win!

The Lonesome Leaf's Lament

Alone on my stem, I sigh with a pout,
Wondering what all the fuss is about.
The others are chatting, all full of cheer,
While I'm just here, feeling oddly severe.

'Why are you sad?' whispers sweet Dracaena,
I shrug and I mumble, 'Just a shy hyena.'
'Come join our fun!' chirps the peppy philodendron,
But I just prefer my quiet retention.

From my perch, I can see a whole leafy scene,
The party's in full swing, oh what could it mean?
But deep down inside, I'm quite fond of the still,
Even a loner can savor a thrill.

So I'll be the wallflower, an old leafy chap,
Enjoying the laughter, a gentle leaf nap.
And maybe one day, I'll join in the fun,
For even the lonesome can sparkle like sun!

Roots of Thought and Reverie

In the corner, I sway and grin,
My roots dig deep, let the fun begin!
Photosynthesizing my thoughts each day,
Where's my coffee? I need it to play.

Chatting with the ants on the ground,
They tell me tales of the world around.
I ponder life under the sun's bright glow,
Is it just me, or is the dirt too slow?

With leaves like hands, I wave to the breeze,
Am I a plant or just a green tease?
A dance with the shadows, a waltz with delight,
Life's a party in the soft, dim light.

So here I stand, in my little pot,
Throwing shade at ideas, quite a lot!
If only the gardener could see my wit,
They'd laugh and say, "Who planted this wit?"

Nature's Inner Dialogue

Every curl of my leaf has a tale to tell,
Whispering secrets that suit me so well.
A chat with the butterflies, oh what a laugh,
Counting their spots like a silly gaffe.

I stretch for the sun, each morning's quest,
Hoping to flourish and be the best.
Do I need a spa day? A little trim?
If I were a cat, I'd have yoga to skim!

I overheard the wind, oh what a funny guy,
Tickling my leaves as he swooshed by.
"Don't worry," he said, "You'll grow ever so tall!"
I replied, "Just as long as I don't hit the wall!"

With every petal, I laugh and I sway,
Nature's banter makes dull days okay.
In my leafy kingdom, let the joy flow,
For a plant's perspective is quite the show!

The Green Heart Speaks

Tick-tock goes the clock, leaves dance around,
I'm the queen here, the true underground.
With roots like stories, all tangled in fun,
I chat with the soil, 'Are we not one?'

My veins are electric, pumping good cheer,
Swaying to rhythms, I'm never unclear.
What's this? A raindrop! A tickle, a tease!
Oh joy, oh glee! Nature's little breeze!

I've got a crush on the sun, it's true,
Bathing in rays, feeling brand new.
The clouds roll by, making faces so bold,
I giggle and wiggle, if only I told!

So if you catch me in a moment so bright,
I'm probably chatting with stars at night.
A green heart whispers, "Life's a fine jest!"
With laughter and leaves, I'm truly blessed!

Between the Pot and the Sky

Here I stand, between earth and sky,
With aspirations that soar oh-so-high.
Little do they know, my leaves hold the key,
To a world of whimsy and glee, oh me!

Passersby wonder, "Is she really alive?"
Oh, if they could hear how my thoughts thrive!
A debate with the sun: who shines the best?
I tell him, "Buddy, it's a leafy fest!"

With the breeze as my buddy and roots as my song,
I chuckle at how everything feels right and wrong.
My pot is my castle, my throne on the floor,
I'm ready for shenanigans and a little bit more!

So plant those feet, and let laughter fly,
Life's a jungle gym, oh my, oh my!
Between the pot and the sky, I'll sway and sway,
For every leaf knows it's a playdate today!

The Poetry of Petioles

In corners of sunlight, I stand so tall,
With leaves that look shiny, I'm here for it all.
Chit-chat with spiders, they're cool little pals,
We giggle at humans who fuss with their gals.

I sway with the breeze; it's a dance, you see,
Pretending I'm waving just so happily.
They marvel my beauty, but can't fathom why,
My pot's full of secrets, I won't tell them why.

I throw shade on the cat who just lounges about,
He leaps like a fool; what's that all about?
As I sip the sunlight and drink in the rain,
I can't stand the way he just snoozes again.

So here in my spot, I'll twirl and I'll twist,
A plant with a passion, I insist I exist!
With laughter and sunlight, I'll lift every gloom,
For life is a party; let's fill up the room!

Dreams in Deep Green

Oh, to be a plant with big dreams, so bright,
Wishing for parties that last through the night.
Bouncing with joy, I create a fine scene,
With vines like confetti, I'm living my dream.

Rubber ducks float in my imaginary sea,
And garden gnomes dance; they're so wild and free!
Each morning I stretch, reaching out for the skies,
I'm blooming in laughter, oh what a surprise!

I secretly plot pranks on the curious pots,
Who fawn over flowers, just tied up in knots.
While they all play nice, I'll twist and I'll twirl,
They'll wonder what's happening; oh, what a swirl!

With breezes and giggles, I thrive in my space,
A party of greenery, don't miss out on the race.
So join in the fun, keep it lighthearted,
In dreams full of green, we're all just getting started!

Urban Jungle Jive

In the heart of the city, I shimmy and sway,
With neighbors like cacti who live day by day.
The traffic's a symphony, honks in a beat,
In this jungle of concrete, I find my own heat.

Oh look at the dancers, they're tall and so spry,
Ferns in their outfits, they twirl and they fly.
I'll join this mad waltz, with my leaves all aflare,
In this bustling tableau, there's joy to share.

The squirrels do a shuffle, the pigeons take flight,
I've got roots in my groove; oh, what a delight!
With cities as stages, we're a green, leafy crew,
In every nook and cranny, we all share the view.

So let's shake up the sidewalks, let's rattle the streets,
I'm the star of the show with my bushy green feats.
With rhythm and laughter, the skyline's our stage,
In this urban oasis, we're dancing through age!

Evergreen Echoes of Emotion

In stillness I ponder, like sages long past,
My leaves whisper softly, each truth unsurpassed.
Anxiety dances, a shadowy friend,
But I'm making a joke, like plants do pretend.

With roots intertwined, my thoughts twist and glide,
As I reach for the sun, I take laughter in stride.
While others may grumble about gray skies above,
I'm here to remind them that green's all about love.

So let's hold a green meeting; the daisies agree,
We'll giggle at troubles, sip tea by the tree.
With echoes of laughter, through branches they roam,
A forest of friendship, we're never alone.

In the hush of the night, as stars twinkle in cheer,
I'll breathe in my joy, let go of all fear.
Through evergreen echoes, emotions take flight,
With fun in the foliage, it all feels so right!

www.ingramcontent.com/pod-product-compliance
Lightning Source LLC
Chambersburg PA
CBHW070318120526
44590CB00017B/2734